Bad Boys of the Book of Mormon
And What They Teach Us

David Swensen Powell

PO Box 221974 Anchorage, Alaska 99522-1974

ISBN 1-888125-48-9

Library of Congress Catalog Card Number: 99-64095

Illustrations of the Bad Boys by Richard A. Cook

Manufactured in the United States of America.

Dedication

Dedicated to my 1997/98 *Book of Mormon* Seminary Class who helped discover the surprising theme of Nephite Bad Boys and the interesting connection between pride, rebellion, apostasy, and "daggers to the heart."

Foreword

"Wickedness never was happiness," (Alma 41:10) is one of the clearest and most obvious teachings in the scriptures. Yet many of us still choose evil. Nephi taught: "It needs be that there is an opposition in all things. If not so ... righteousness could not be brought to pass, neither wickedness, neither holiness, nor misery, neither good nor bad." (2 Nephi 2:11). This book, *Bad Boys of the Book Mormon* ... and What They Teach Us!, exposes how the adversary works to destroy lives. Through their mistakes, we may gain the wisdom and desire to not choose evil and the way of the adversary.

The word adversary means "one who acts contrary to another's purpose." It is a title of an opponent. Lucifer, intent on destroying the purposes of God, becomes the adversary. In fact, the word Satan comes from the Hebrew saw-tawn, which means to "lie in wait, to oppose, to be an adversary," and thus was applied to the devil. These bad boys of the *Book of Mormon* believe they are wise, but are deceived into becoming spokesmen and representatives of the adversary. They teach us much about Lucifer's techniques, his reasoning, his deceptive practices, and his evil nature.

Time and again it is proven, through these deceived men, that Satan will not support us in their time of need, but will rejoice in our time of pain as he tries to drag us into his domain.

David Powell, through impeccable research and creativity, weaves a tapestry of temptation using the bad boys in the *Book of Mormon*. Political unrest, government corruption, assassinations, bloody wars, moral decay, pride, greed, and unspeakable evil, all are revealed within, showing clearly how the *Book of Mormon* is indeed a work for us in these latter days. David makes it possible for anyone to understand what is in store for those who decide or allow themselves to be a Bad Boy (or Girl) in these times.

This book is a must for Seminary students and teachers, Institute students and teachers, Sunday School students and teachers, and anyone else who is seeking truth. "Choose ye this day whom ye will serve." (Alma 30:8) This book makes clear, with great originality and ingenuity, what happens to those who choose evil.

You can read it in one sitting for the pure enjoyment or you can take your time and underline the numerous stories and applications. Either way, you will find it interesting, informative, and intriguing.

E. Donald Ainge

Table of Contents

Why write a book about bad boys? Isn't that a bit morbid? Aren't we supposed to shun evil? Can we really learn anything from wicked men?

Why is the geography of the *Book of Mormon* so confusing? Where did all this take place anyway? A real simplified map. It doesn't have to be that complicated.

Did you know the *Book of Mormon* covers a 3,000-year history, but 66% of the verses cover only 7% of that time period? Did you know every Record Keeper was a Nephite (except Ether)? Did you know 7% of the book covers 66% of the timeline? Did you know that 16/17 of the Bad Boys all lived 100 years before the coming of Christ? A cool chart.

The Nephites are not the good boys. The Lamanites are not the bad boys. The term "Nephites" does not mean "direct descendants of Nephi" and the term "Lamanites" does not mean the "direct descendants of Laman". All of the "Bad Boys" who are "named" in the *Book of Mormon* are actually "Nephites" or Jaredites. There are no "bad" Lamanites named in the entire *Book of Mormon*.

What happens when people lose their faith in God and begin to think they can do it all on their own? What happens when ambition rules over practicality, hatred over love, vanity over humility, pride over service, war over peace? What happens to people when they become blinded by vengeance, consumed with revenge, and drunk with power? The answers lie in the disappointing lives of four Nephite men who abandon their families, become traitors to their country and reject their God. Although all four men are given an opportunity to change their minds, soften their hearts and repent of their foolishness, each chooses to plunge forward in their sins. Each chooses blood over peace. The consequences of these actions are surprisingly predictable and predictably pathetic.

The Three Run-a-ways 10
What happens to spoiled church members who become offended? Why do people have such a hard time not getting their way? What happens when we have an extreme "all or nothing" disposition? Three of the Nephite villains could be grouped together as tantrum throwing run-a-ways. Their stubborn attitudes, rebellious hearts, and proud spirits cause them to abandon their faith, run away from their problems, and try and live separate lives from their families, from their country, and from their religion. These three dissenters all die in dramatic fashion, answering the question, "Is it really so wrong to just do what I want?"

The Four Silver Spoons 14
There is a well-known phenomenon in the church called the Bishop's Son Syndrome. It is unfairly labeled since it

happens to all kinds of families, not just the Bishop's. The theory goes that sons of a Bishop have too much of a good thing and rebel. They have the gospel, they have good parents, they are born to privilege, they have been taught the truth, they have silver spoons stuck in their mouth and all they have to do is be obedient. However, there are many such people who, with very little excuse for not believing, reject the teachings of their parents, apostatize from the church and seek their own dead-end paths. There are four such "Bad Boys" in the *Book of Mormon* who fit in this category. They had the truth, the power, the position, the respect, and they abused all of it. Their corruption, fall, and attempts at repentance (or lack there of), are fascinating.

There are two kinds of Hypocrites. The first kind is the most popular. It could be called, "Good on the outside, Bad on the inside." Some of us pretend to be good. We go to church, we sit on the bench, and we smile at our neighbor. However, on the inside, we don't have a testimony, we don't have spiritual conviction, and we are only reluctantly going through the motions of being good. Since we have not internalized any conviction to do what God wants us to do, when no one is looking we sin, sin, sin. — The other kind of hypocrite is just the opposite. Internally, in our heart of hearts, in our souls, in our minds, we know what is right. We know what God expects of us and we know the consequences of our actions. We believe the words of the prophets and have felt of God's Love. However, our actions tell a different story. To be seen of others, to attain popularity, to gain friends or position, we choose to rebel against our convictions, reject our morals, and hopelessly justify our actions to some fruitless end. Three of the *Book of Mormon* villains fall into this second category. On the inside they know what is right, but on the outside, they tell a different story. Their unfortunate demise is shocking. God will not be mocked. Two are struck by God's power and eventually die. One is killed by the state for his capital crimes.

Three Dangerous Hypocrites 23
There are two kinds of hypocrites (see above). The first kind of hypocrite pretends to be good on the outside, but is really bad on the inside. Three of the Bad Boys of the *Book of Mormon* fit into this category. Through their secret promises, secret meetings, and secret acts, they walk through the city streets pretending to be believers. However, they are two-faced, conniving cowards. They are complete "Pretenders". They covet political power and control. They hate authority, yet want authority over others. All three murder other men in cold-blood. They are personally taught secret blood oaths and death promises (secret combinations) by Satan himself. This kind of hypocrite is the more sinister of the two. This kind of rogue proves to be the cause of the entire destruction of the Nephite Nation (almost).

Preface

Wow! What a strange idea! A whole book focusing on the villains in the *Book of Mormon*. I know what you are probably thinking, "Why write a book about the bad people in the *Book of Mormon*? Shouldn't we spend more time focusing on the teachings of the prophets, the high priests, righteous kings, and faithful missionaries in the *Book of Mormon* and dismiss the villains?"

Well, most people do gloss over the Bad Boys. However, I think the lessons we learn from the scoundrels in the *Book of Mormon* are fascinating and important for our spiritual growth. Not only that, they are instructional! If nothing else, they illustrate to us what happens to people when they fall away from the church, think they know more than God, allow pride to control their lives, and put themselves, and their wants above those of others, their country, their church, and their family.

Have you ever stopped to think why The *Book of Mormon* (the religious history of a nation) dwells so much on those men who tried to corrupt God's way and pervert the heart's of the people? If one or two villains were mentioned in the *Book of Mormon*, I could dismiss that as insignificant. If 8-10 ruffians were introduced, chronicled, and discussed I would think that a bit odd. What if I told you more bad boys are mentioned in the *Book of Mormon* during a two hundred-year period than are Nephite Prophets in a 1000-year time-period? Well it is true! In fact, it could be argued that the *Book of Mormon* is more a book about how **not to act,** than it is **how to act**.

In Sunday School we learn all about the fabulous miracles of the prophets and miraculous adventures of the missionaries. What about the bad boys? We rarely pause to look at it from the villain's point of view. This Bad Guy Book is about people in the *Book of Mormon* who fall away from the church; their struggles, their justifications, their philosophies, their apostasy, their fears, and their evil designs.

The more I read the *Book of Mormon*, the more I am convinced that this book isn't about Nephites or Lamanites.... It is about you and me. The ancient text is about normal church members struggling to keep the commandments. Some of us strive to be popular, some strive to be powerful, some strive to be rich, some of us strive to excel in community issues, and some are consumed with lust for another, etc. Just because we were baptized at some point in our life does not immunize us from being attracted to these powerful emotions and desires.

The forward of the *Book of Mormon* says its purpose is to bring both Jew and Gentile to the knowledge that Jesus is the Christ. I believe a second purpose is to teach both Jew and Gentile (once they have joined the church) the treachery of the adversary, the danger signs of apostasy and the pitfalls of false doctrine. The *Book of Mormon* is a veritable blueprint for members of what not to do, what not to think, and what not to be, if they want to grow closer to the star of the book, Jesus Christ.

The purpose of this Bad Guy Book is to look closely at the villains and see what they have to teach us.

- Why did Mormon include them in the sacred records?
- What is their message?
- Do they have anything in common?
- Can I learn anything from wicked men?

I hope as you read this book, you will come to see the genius of Mormon's writings and seriously ponder the challenging rhetoric these shysters illustrate. If my hunch is right, you may not only be able to recognize some of your own shortcomings and faults through reading this book, but you will also see the consequences the villains bring upon themselves, thus causing you to recommit yourself to obeying God's commandments.

Bad Boys
Geography

To better understand the comings and goings of our *Book of Mormon* hooligans, there are a few geographical points I wish to summarize, so as to make this book more reader-friendly.

Having taught seminary for many years, I know *Book of Mormon* geography can be complicated and confusing for the average student. There are lands Northward, lands Southward, lands to the East, lands by the seashore, the Land of Desolation, the Narrow Neck of Land, the Land of our First Inheritance, the Land of the Lamanites, the Land of Nephi, and too many other cities and rivers to even try to name.

For the purposes of this book, there are only three simple geographic concepts the reader needs to understand.

1. The Land of Nephi
- The land of Nephi is also called the Land of our First Inheritance.
- The Land of Nephi is where Nephi and his family first landed. (Like Plymouth Rock.)
- The Nephites eventually abandoned the Land of Nephi, leaving only Lamanites in the land southward.
- The Land of Nephi is actually where the Lamanites live.
- The Land of Nephi is to the South of Zara-hemla (see map on next page).

2. Zarahemla
- Zarahemla is the city founded by the Mulekites.
- Mosiah stumbled upon this city in 200 BC.
- The Nephites merge with the Mulekites.
- Zarahemla becomes the principal Nephite City.
- Zarahemla is to the North of the Land of Nephi (see map below).

3. Nobody Really Knows
- Nobody knows the actual location of the *Book of Mormon* lands.
- The Church has never published any official statement saying that the *Book of Mormon* took place in Central America, or anywhere else for that matter.
- Many people believe that South America is the Land Southward, Central America is the Narrow Neck of Land, and that North America is the Land Northward. Nobody really knows!

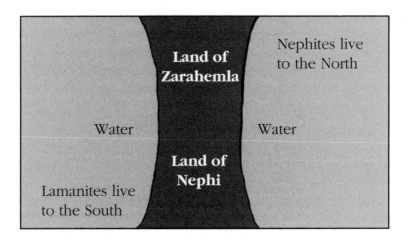

Interesting Time Line Facts

Now we have simplified the map where the villains are going to be plotting their evil plans, let me also simplify the *Book of Mormon* timeline. One of the most interesting points brought to light when talking about the Bad Boys is the fact that all of the villains in the *Book of Mormon* live and die during the 100 year period just prior to the coming of Christ to the Americas. (Except for Sherem and not including the Jaredites.)

In other words, from the time Lehi lands in America to 100 BC (500 years), the only rogue in the *Book of Mormon* text is the anti-Christ, Sherem.

During the 450 years after Christ, there are no scalawags mentioned. All bad people during this period are lumped together as generic Lamanites.

Therefore, this bad guy book will almost exclusively be talking about the time period 100 BC-33 AD.

- And although the *Book of Mormon* covers a 3,000-year period, 66% of the verses in the *Book of Mormon* cover only a 200-year period.
- The chart on the next page also reveals 66% of the verses cover only 7% of the time line and 7% of the verses cover 66% of the time line. In addition, we see that every Record Keeper in the *Book of Mormon* was a Nephite (except for Ether, of course).

Record Keeper	Start Year	End Year	Total Years	Verses Written	Gives Plates To	Relationship
Ether	2200	200	2000	433	Limhi	King Who Finds Plates
Nephi	600	544	56	1268	Jacob	Brother
Jacob	544	500	44	203	Enos	Son
Enos	500	420	80	27	Jarom	Son
Jarom	420	361	59	15	Omni	Son
Omni	361	317	44	3	Ammaron	Son
Ammaron	317	279	38	5	Chemish	Brother
Chemish	279	200	79	1	Abinadon	Son
Abinadon	200	150	50	2	Amaleki	Son
Amaleki	150	130	20	18	Benjamin	None-The King
Benjamin	130	124	6	135	Mosiah	Son
Mosiah	124	90	34	167	Alma II	None-High Priest's Son
Alma II	90	73	17	1363	Helaman	Son
Helaman	73	57	16	590	Shiblon	Son
Shiblon	57	53	4	7	Helaman	Brother
Helaman	54	39	14	85	Nephi	Son
Nephi	39	0	39	412	Nephi	Son
Nephi	1	38	36	785	Nephi	Son
Nephi	36	136	100	14	Amos	Son
Amos	136	220	86	1	Amos	Son
Amos	220	305	85	24	Ammoron	Son
Ammoron	305	322	17	2	Mormon	Neighbor Boy
Mormon	345	385	40	216	Moroni	Son
Moroni	385	421	36	182	Joseph Smith	Neighbor Boy
TOTALS			**3000**	**5958**		

Book of Mormon Myths

*Now we have established the map and the timeline,
there are three myths which must be cleared up to better
understand these apostate degenerates.*

MYTH NUMBER ONE
The Nephites are the Good Boys!

If you were asked to give a thumbnail summary of the
Book of Mormon to a nonmember, what would you say?
How would you start? Perhaps you would say what most
missionaries say.

In fact, it was while sitting in a recent missionary discussion
I decided to write this book. The Elder began, "The *Book
of Mormon* is basically a history of two civilizations; The
Nephites and The Lamanites. The Nephites are generally
the good boys and the Lamanites are generally the bad
boys...." Do you agree so far? Most members would. It is
easy to explain and easy to understand. However, it
couldn't be farther from the truth.

First of all, the Nephites were not good!
- Yes, they had the prophets among them.
- Yes, they had the true teachings.
- Yes, some of them honored their priesthood.

- Yes, many of them were members of God's church.

Nevertheless, as a people, as a nation, they were a wicked and rebellious group. They were proud, selfish, self-centered, and had ridiculously short memories. Even the church was in a constant struggle between mild apostasy and total apostasy. When they weren't casting out the poor and the sick, they were puffing themselves up with jewelry, costly apparel, and ramiumptums. If they weren't fighting Lamanites, they were warring among themselves.[1]

From the time Nephi left Jerusalem to the coming of Christ (approximately 600 years) we read story after story of rebellious church members who fall into apostasy, reject their church leaders, stone the prophets, and curse God. In fact, can you name one extended period of time in that 600 year period when the Nephites were righteous? Wouldn't you agree, with a few pockets of exception (Alma 50:23), the Nephites as a nation are generally in a constant state of rebellion, wickedness, and disobedience?

Consider two examples of the Nephites as a corrupt nation. First, when Christ was crucified, the Nephite nation was destroyed because of their wickedness (3 Ne 8-10). The destruction was devastating. Only a "few of the more righteous" survived (Helaman 6:1). Secondly, consider the end of the *Book of Mormon*. In the end, we read that the Nephites were more wicked than the Lamanites. In fact, God allowed the Lamanites to destroy the Nephites because of their exceedingly great wickedness. Only 14 Nephites (out of a million+) were spared. (See Mormon 1:1, Moroni 2:3)

[1] See Jacob 3:3; Enos 1:22; Alma 53:8; Helaman 3:33-34; Helaman 6:18-21; 4 Ne 1:17,43-45; Helaman 6:34; Helaman 4:11-13; 3 Nephi 7:2; Mormon 3:9-11; Moroni 9.

There were some good Nephites, but to say the Nephites were the good boys simply is not true!

Interestingly, only three women are named in the entire *Book of Mormon*. Two are Nephites, yet not stellar examples of faithful women. One is a Lamanite and is a stellar example of a faithful believer in Christ.

- Sariah—A Nephite woman, who whined, complained, doubted, called her husband a visionary man, lacked faith in God and was for the most part a lukewarm member.
- Isabel—A Nephite prostitute who slept with Corianton, the prophet's son.
- Abish—A faithful Lamanite woman who was converted in her youth and single handedly helped thousands of Lamanites come unto Christ (with Ammon's help).

MYTH NUMBER TWO
The Lamanites are the bad boys!

This myth is only partially true. First of all, can you name a bad Lamanite in the *Book of Mormon*? Go ahead, pick one.

What about Gadianton? Nope, he was a Nephite apostate.

How about King Noah and his wicked priests? Nope. His people were Nephites from the land of Zarahemla (Mosiah 11:16-19).

Well, surely the three anti-Christs, Korihor, Nehor, and Sherem, were wicked Lamanites. Right? Nope! All three were most likely living in the land where the Nephites lived and were most likely fair-skinned Nephites (See Terminology Page and Alma 30:18, Index: Nehor (2), See Sherem-Chapter 3).

The same can be said for other notable villains like Zeezrom, Kishkumen, Amalickiah, Zarahemnah, and Amlici. Even minor wicked people named in the book are not Lamanites at all, but are apostate Nephites. Zoram, Morianton, Corianton, Seantum, Ammoron, and Isabel the Harlot, are all Nephites gone bad.

In fact, there is not a single bad Lamanite mentioned in the entire *Book of Mormon* text. The Lamanites who are named in the *Book of Mormon* are actually converts to the church of God or Nephite sympathizers. They certainly are not bad boys.

> Samual the Lamanite—Convert
> King Lamoni—Lamanite Convert
> King Lamoni's father—Lamanite Convert
> 2000 Stripling Warriors—Lamanite Teenagers

Many heroes of the *Book of Mormon* are actually the so-called Bad Boys. In addition to those mentioned above, the Anti-Nephi-Lehies are also famous Lamanites, but they are only famous because of their miraculous conversion to the church of God. They become Nephites.

There were wicked Lamanites. I am not saying the Lamanite nation was not a bloodthirsty, hostile problem for the Nephites. What I am saying is the *Book of Mormon* is not about Lamanites. Those Lamanites who do happen to get mentioned and talked about in the *Book of Mormon* were actually good.

Nephites wrote the *Book of Mormon* about Nephites (or

Nephite converts). Lamanites are mentioned only when they are converted en-masse, or lumped together as the attacking armies. To say the *Book of Mormon* is about two nations; the Lamanites and the Nephites; is kind of like saying the history of England is about two nations; England and Ireland.

MYTH NUMBER THREE
Nephites are descendants of Nephi and Lamanites are descendants of Laman!

Contrary to popular belief, a Nephite can be more than "a direct descendant of Nephi, son of Lehi." In fact, the word Nephite is used in many different connotations. Sometimes it is used to describe all people who are under the King who governs the Nephites (believers and nonbelievers—See Jacob 1-7). Sometimes it describes "the people of God." Other times it simply describes the people who "are not Lamanites." In other words, the term appears as a socio-political title more than it ever refers to "Nephites as direct descendants of Nephi." The word Nephite appears 382 times, "people of the Nephites" appears 18 times, People of Nephi appears four times, children of Nephi appears twice, and "descendants of Nephi" only appears twice.

The same can be said for the Lamanites. The term Lamanites refers to those people who were not Nephites. Sometimes it refers to those in opposition to the Church of God, sometimes it refers to those who lived in the land of Nephi. The word appears 700-plus times, but only once does it refer to "direct descendants of Laman." The two terms (Lamanite and Nephite) are not meant to denote a genealogical or ethnic heritage.

For example, in Jacob 1:3 he says in order to make things

more simple, Jacob is just going to use the term Lamanite to lump together all of the many different tribes and peoples who were not Nephites or people who followed the teachings of Christ.

In Mosiah 25:13, we read that the Nephites joined the Mulekites in the city of Zarahemla. Shortly after that time, Mosiah refers to all of the people in Zarahemla as Nephites.

In Mosiah 25:12 the people of Ammon (the Anti-Nephi Lehies) want to take upon them the title of Nephites. The term was widely used as a label, not to denote a particular heritage.

After Christ's appearance to the Nephites, we read there were no longer "ites" among them. However, the minute a portion of the people apostatized from the true order of God, they are called Lamanites (see 4 Ne 1:1-35). Obviously, this does not mean they are all direct descendants of Laman. It simply means they were no longer considered to be among the Nephites. However, these "Nephites" were soon more wicked than the Lamanites. In other words, Nephite was not another word for Good and Lamanite was not synonymous with Bad. There were good people and bad people on both sides.

THREE MYTH SUMMARY

- The term Nephite is a socio-political term, not a genealogical/ethnic term.
- The term Lamanite is a socio-political term, not a genealogical/ethnic term.
- The Nephites were just as wicked as the Lamanites (most of the time).

- Nephites wrote the *Book of Mormon*, about Nephites (or converts to Nephites).
- There are no bad Lamanites named in the *Book of Mormon*.
- The only villains in the *Book of Mormon* are Nephites or Jaredites.
- This book highlights the bad Nephites and what happens to them.

Amalickiah

One of Four Nephite Military Dissenters

Alma 46-51

Born: Circa 50 BC
Raised: Zarahemla
Religion: Probably was taught the Law of Moses.
Nationality: Nephite. (Alma 48:25)
Profession: Political wannabe. Military leader. Cunning traitor.
Major Sins: Pride. Lust for power. Murder. Total apostasy.
Repented: No
Result: A javelin was thrust through his heart while he lay sleeping in his tent.

Summary of Amalickiah

The story of Amalickiah is barely believable. This guy is the epitome of good timing and taking advantage of that good timing. Amalickiah goes from being a Nephite political loser to King of the Lamanites. It is one story that is exciting reading and fascinating literature.

Amalickiah has a high need for power and a high need to control others. He wants to be king over the Nephites.

He runs for the Chief Judge position. He loses. He sulks. He speaks out against the government. He plots to overthrow the government. Captain Moroni finds out about it and comes to squelch the uprising (Alma 46:3). Not even Amalickiah is dumb enough to go up against Moroni. He and his brother (Ammoron) and their political loyalists flee the land of Zarahemla and head south toward the Land of Nephi (where the Lamanites live).

Having just been in a very bloody war with the Lamanites, the last thing Moroni wants is for some whiny Nephite traitors going over there with fresh apostate troops bent on destroying the Nephites. So Moroni pursues them and captures most of them. Amalickiah and his brother get away and make it to the land of the Nephites. Now this is where the story gets really dicey (Alma 46:28).

Amalickiah actually stirs the Lamanite King into a frenzy and persuades him to commit the entire Lamanite army to go to war against Moroni. The king issues a war proclamation. However, the Lamanite army is divided. Half are loyal to the king. Half are scared of Captain Moroni. They refuse to fight. This disobedience enrages the king. The king actually puts Amalickiah (a Nephite) in charge of the half of the army who is loyal to the king and commands him to fight the half who is scared to go up against Moroni.

In a bizarre twist of events, Amalickiah becomes friends with the leader of the scared army. His name is Lehonti. He tells the scared Lehonti if he will put Amalickiah as his second in command of all the troops, he will allow Lehonti to sneak up on the loyalists' camp during the night and capture them without bloodshed. Lehonti agrees. Amalickiah surrenders his troops to Lehonti and Amalickiah is placed as second in command. The Lamanite army is once again united. (Alma 47:10-19)

The plot thickens when Amalickiah has Lehonti secretly poisoned. Once Lehonti dies, naturally Amalickiah becomes the leader of the Lamanite Army. (Alma 47:35) Unbelievable, right?! Just wait.

Next, Amalickiah leads the united army back to the Land of Nephi. The king comes out to greet them. Amalickiah sends a few of his henchmen ahead to meet the king. After kneeling before the king and kissing his hand, one of the henchmen stabs the king and then blames it on the king's servants. The servants run, thus looking guilty. By the time Amalickiah returns to the Lamanite capital, the queen is pleading with him to not destroy the city with her own army. To make things even more bizarre, Amalickiah becomes quite enamored with the Lamanite queen and they soon marry.

Therefore, Amalickiah not only connives and murders his way to military leadership, but he also connives and murders his way to be the political leader. Unbelievable!

Guess what his first royal decree is? Kill all Nephites! (Alma 48:1) The reenergized Lamanites, with their Nephite king agree to go to battle against Moroni. (This is where Moroni raises the title of liberty, etc.) Their battles are terrible. They fight all day in the blistering tropical sun. One night, Chief Captain Teancum has had enough. He takes matters into his own hands and in an unbelievable act of his own, he sneaks into the Lamanite camp in the middle of the night, finds Amalickiah's teepee, sneaks in and thrusts a javelin through his heart so expertly, Amalickiah doesn't even groan. (Alma 51:34) Teancum escapes unnoticed and the

Lamanites awake with the terrible discovery that their king and general has been slain. Thus is the quick rise and quick fall of a two-bit Nephite traitor.

His younger brother, Ammoron, becomes king (more on him later).

What we learn from Amalickiah

We learn "the great wickedness one very wicked man can cause to take place among the children of men." We also see that because he was, "a man of cunning device and a man of many flattering words, he led away the hearts of many people to do wickedness; yea and to seek to destroy the church of God, and to destroy the foundation of liberty, which thing God had granted unto them."

- We also learn how fragile freedom is and how fragile governments are.
- We also learn how vain and foolish the pursuit of power really is.
- But we learn to what ends an ambitious man will go to get what he wants.

Personal Application

- Are you humble?
- Do you take council easily?
- Or do you harden your heart and rebel against God?
- Do you flatter your friends and family into talking badly against your church leaders and political leaders?
- Would your friends generally consider you a conniver?
- Are you sleeping with the enemy to make a point? Are you reckless in the pursuit of your

so-called dreams at the expense of your family and loved ones?

Thoughts

Amalickiah is a classic example that the *Book of Mormon* is about bad Nephites, not bad Lamanites. This story is really about what happens to a church member when he forsakes his religion and pursues vain and foolish lusts. Amalickiah could be any of us, if we allow our pride to consume us. How often are we offended? How often are we embarrassed in front of others? How do we handle these trying events? Do we curse God or do we humbly take it in stride and learn from it.

Amalickiah

Yea, we see that Amalickiah, because he was a man of cunning device and a man of many flattering words, that he led away the hearts of many people to do wickedly; yea, and to seek to destroy the church of God, and to destroy the foundation of liberty which God had granted unto them, or which blessing God had sent upon the face of the land for the righteous' sake.

Alma 46:10

2

Ammoron

One of Four Nephite Military Dissenters

Born: Circa 50 BC
Raised: In the Nephite Capital, Zarahemla.
Religion: Jewish apostate.
Nationality: Nephite
Profession: Military leader.
Major Sins: Pride. Unrepentant heart. Going along with his brother's foolish ideas of grandeur.
Repented: No
Result: Javelin through his heart while sleeping in his teepee.

Summary of Ammoron

Ammoron is the brother of Amalickiah. He assumes the military lead of the Lamanite army when Amalickiah is slain by Teancum. His life mirrors that of his brother. He is with Amalickiah when he runs for office and loses. He is there at the treason meetings. He is there when Amalickiah runs from Moroni. He is there when Amalickiah escapes to the Lamanites. He is there at the wedding of the Lamanite queen and his brother. He goes to battle by Amalickiah's side. He could have been the one who found his brother's body. He succeeds his brother's military prominence. He followed in his big brother's footsteps. He even died the same way his brother did.

The Nephites, hoping the Lamanites would lose courage with Amalickiah's death, were saddened to learn Amalickiah's brother, Ammoron, swore revenge on them for the cold-blooded murder of his brother. The battles continue for a season. Teancum figures if it worked once, maybe it will work again. He sneaks into their camp. He finds the teepee of Ammoron and uses another trusty javelin and strikes Ammoron right through the heart. This time, however, Teancum is caught and slain. Thus ends the life of a Nephite patriot and a Nephite traitor, all in the same night.

What we learn from Ammoron

The obvious teaching we learn from this Nephite bad-boy is the danger of following family members and not following God. The saying goes that blood is thicker than water. Ammoron's loyalty may be admirable, but it is tragically misguided. We should be loyal to the blood of Christ, with which we were purchased. He should be our example and leader, no matter how much we admire a brother or a spouse. If they do not follow the teachings of Christ, they are not to be followed. Christ is the way the truth and the life. His blood is thicker than our pathetic, misguided, proud, and overzealous support of a cor-rupted family member.

Personal Application

Are you alive with your own flame of testimony or are you depending on the light of others? Are you able to discern false teachings, even if they come from a loved one? Is your loyalty to the savior, even over your love of a sibling or a parent? In a weird, backward kind of way, this story can inspire us if we are as loyal to Christ as Ammoron was to his brother, Amalickiah; through thick and thin, hard times and good times, through defeat and victory, through life and death.

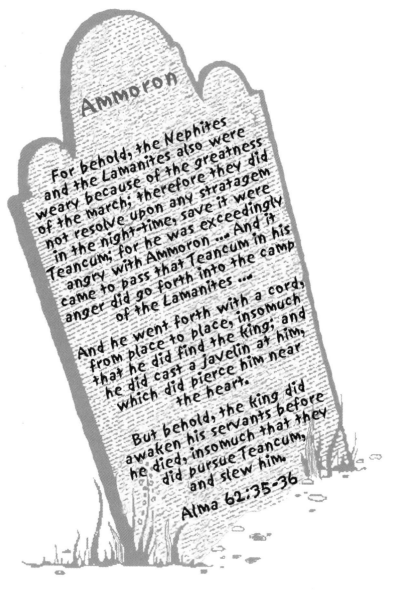

Ammoron

For behold, the Nephites and the Lamanites also were weary because of the greatness of the march; therefore they did not resolve upon any stratagem in the night-time, save it were Teancum; for he was exceedingly angry with Ammoron ... And it came to pass that Teancum in his anger did go forth into the camp of the Lamanites ...

And he went forth with a cord, from place to place, insomuch that he did find the king; and he did cast a javelin at him, which did pierce him near the heart.

But behold, the king did awaken his servants before he died, insomuch that they did pursue Teancum, and slew him.

Alma 62:35-36

3

Zarahemnah

One of Four Nephite Military Dissenters

Alma 43-44

Born: Circa 74 BC
Raised: Not stated.
Religion: Anti-Christian.
Nationality: This is somewhat debatable. He is the leader of the Lamanite army. However, the Lamanites generally put Nephites or Zoramites or other non-Lamanites at the head of their armies. He knew the language of Captain Moroni. He was well versed in the teachings of the Nephites. The *Book of Mormon* text never says what nationality he is. Precedence would suggest he is not a dark skinned Lamanite.
Profession: Military Leader.
Major Sins: Back-stabbing, stubborn, proud man.
Repented: Kinda, but not really.
Result: Many of his soldiers were killed. He finally surrenders.

Summary of Zarahemnah

Zarahemnah is a large and mighty leader. Unfortunately, he had never fought against Captain Moroni. After several small defeats to Moroni, Zarahemnah swears to drink

Moroni's blood, if he ever gets the chance. In the next battle, Moroni surrounds Zarahemnah with his army and tells Zarahemnah to throw down his weapons, make a covenant never to return to battle against the Nephites, and to leave in peace or die. Zarahemnah proposes a different set of conditions. He will leave in peace, he will throw down his weapons, but he won't make a pact which he knows he will break. He wants to come again against Moroni in the future. (Alma 44:15)

Moroni tells Zarahemnah that he is in no position to change the surrender conditions and if he does not follow all three conditions, Moroni will command his army to attack from all sides and slaughter the Lamanites. Zarahemnah throws a temper tantrum during this face-to-face meeting with Moroni and tries to leap forward and kill Moroni. One of Moroni's guards steps forward and scalps Zarahemnah. Still, Zarahemnah will not surrender. He commands his men to fight. Some do and die. The rest make the covenant. Zarahemnah eventually agrees also and departs back down to the land of Nephi, never to be heard of again.

What we learn from Zarahemnah
- We learn that when you are surrounded by an army of armor plated men carrying very sharp steel swords and they offer you the opportunity to peacefully surrender, you should surrender.
- We learn that God helps those who help themselves.
- We learn that the stubborn characters of wicked men can throw entire nations into war.
- We learn that God will not be mocked.
- We learn that if you throw tantrums, you just might lose your scalp (ouch).

Personal Application

- Do you pick and choose which command-ments you will follow?
- Do you only obey after hitting rock bottom?
- Are you so proud, and so hard, that you mock God with your behavior?
- Do others honor your word? Are you a Man of Your Word?
- Do you look for God's hand in your life, or do you walk around in denial?

Thoughts

This story reminds me of the war in heaven. God presents his plan. We can either accept or reject it. Satan offers a totally different plan. God did not ask for a better plan, or a different plan. He asked us if we wanted to follow it or not follow it. Zarahemnah offered a different plan than the one presented to him by Moroni, just like Lucifer presented a different plan to God.

Since we are here on earth, we have already agreed to follow Jesus Christ. That decision has already been made. Now, let's get out there and do it!

Zarahemnah
Now this he did that he might preserve their hatred towards the Nephites, that he might bring them into subjection to the accomplish-ment of his designs. For be-hold, his designs were to be-did that the Lamanites to anger against the Nephites; this he power over them, usurp great that he might them, and also the Nephites by bringing them into bondage.
Alma 43:7-8

4

Coriantumr

One of Four Nephite Military Dissenters

Helaman 1

Born: Circa 51 BC
Raised: Zarahemla
Religion: Unknown
Nationality: Mulekite/Nephite dissenter
Profession: Military Leader
Major Sins: Proud. High need for power. Bloodthirsty.
Repented: No
Result: Killed in battle.

Summary of Coriantumr

Very little is known about Coriantumr. The *Book of Mormon* text is, however, very specific in denoting his nationality. Like most all of the Lamanite military leaders, he is not a Lamanite. He is a direct descendant of Zarahemla (the Mulekite). Somewhere along the line he leaves his childhood home and dissents down to the land of Nephi to live with the Lamanites. His dislike for Zarahemla and his family is not an idle falling out. When he is made Chief Captain over an innumerable army of Lamanites, he spares no time in leading the army right to the stairs of the Zarahemla Capital and takes the city (personally killing Pacumeni, the Nephite Chief Judge).

This would be like Jimmy Carter invading Washington DC with an Iraqi army and moving into the White House (where he used to live). Coriantumr's storming the capital is quite amazing at first glance. The Nephites did not defend this "inner city" because they thought it would be ridiculous for any army to attack the heart of the Nephite Nation. Coriantumr marched right into the heart of the Nephites and took the crown jewel. His triumph was remarkable. He toppled the great Nephite city without hardly breaking a sweat.

Somewhat discouraged by the ease of his triumph, or drunk with blood and power, he makes a tactical error. He keeps going. He starts attacking other nearby cities. He is successful at first. But just like in the game of *Risk*, it is always fun when it is your turn, but when you spread your armies too thin, and the other guy now has a chance to mount an offensive, it suddenly isn't fun anymore.

That is what happens to Coriantumr. He spread his armies thin right in the heart of the Nephite nation. After recovering from the shock of the initial invasion, the Nephites wage a counterattack. Coriantumr is surrounded on all sides by Nephites. Coriantumr tries to retreat, but he retreats into more Nephites. Coriantumr is slain.

What we learn from Coriantumr
- We learn that pride can cause you to make really foolish decisions.
- We learn that it is best to stay away from people with a high need for power.
- We learn that hatred can blind you into

plunging your army into a ridiculously perilous position.

- We learn that putting overzealous ex-Nephites, who have an ax to grind with their motherland, may not be the wisest choice for military leader.
- When you have a fight with your mom and dad, attacking them with the neighbor's army is a mistake.

Personal Application

- Are you like Coriantumr?
- Have you dissented from your childhood teachings?
- Do you think you know it all?
- Just because you have a lot of friends, do you now want to show your parents how mature you are?
- Isn't it about time to repent of your pride and reconcile with your family before someone gets hurt?

Thoughts

Those with home-field advantage really do have it! Stay home!

Coriantumr

But it came to pass that Coriantumr did march forth at the head of his numerous host, and came upon the inhabitants of the city, and their march was with such exceedingly great speed that there was no time for the Nephites to gather together their armies. And it came to pass that Moronihah did head them in their retreat, and did give unto them battle, insomuch that it became an exceedingly bloody battle; yea, many were slain; and among the number who were slain Coriantumr was also found.

Helaman 1:19,30

5

Zoram
One of Three Run-a-ways

Born: Circa 74 BC
Raised: Probably in Zarahemla. Later he moved himself and his followers to Antionum, which was a Nephite city east of Sidom
Religion: This guy was a true apostate, in every sense of the word. He rejected Jesus completely.
Nationality: Nephite/Zoramite.
Profession: Political leader and preacher.
Major Sins: Total apostasy. Rebellion. Idol worship. Unrepentant. Proud. Murder. Treason.
Repented:: No
Result: Death unknown.

Summary of Zoram

Little is known about Zoram's childhood, his parentage or his death. However, we learn of the consequences of his life and teachings he had among people. Basically, we know Zoram was a Nephite man who, at some point, decided to reject the Law of Moses and persuaded a bunch of people to do the same. He then took the people east of Zarahemla to a city near the border with the Lamanites and set up a new colony, (Antionum). It was there in the new colony Zoram taught the people a "New Gospel" according to how he wanted things to be. He taught some truths. However, he only mingled the scriptures into his own philosophies.

This rebellion and rejection of the true order of God could have severe consequences. Alma was perplexed. He did not want the Zoramites to fall away from the truth or to join with the Lamanites, so Alma put together a power-house group of missionaries to go over to the land of Zoram to try to teach them the truth and to persuade them to come back to Zarahemla. Alma knew the word of God was more powerful than the sword. So he took with him some of the best missionaries in the *Book of Mormon*; three of the four sons of Mosiah (including Ammon), Amulek, Zeezrom, and he also brings two of his own sons, Corianton and Shiblon.

When they arrive, they go directly to the synagogue. What they find is total blasphemy and apostasy. First thing they see is a giant alter/tower where each person goes to pray. The prayers are set and repeated verbatim. We catch a glimpse of Zoram's pride and puffed-up heart in these prayers, which is extremely sorrowful to the missionary group. Here is a sample of what the prayers contained: (Picture this being yelled from a tall tower so all could hear. I don't think someone could sit down today and write a more self-centered, self-aggrandizing, self-ab-sorbed, proud prayer if they tried.)

"Holy God, we believe that thou has separated us from our brethren; and we do not believe in the traditions of our brethren, which was handed down to them by the childishness of their fathers; but we believe that

*thou hast elected us to be thy holy children; and also
hast made it known to us that there shall be no Christ
... and thou hast elected us that we shall be saved,
whilst all around us elected to be cast by thy wrath
down to hell ... we also thank thee that thou has elected
us, that we may not be led away by the foolish traditions of our brethren, which doth bind them down to
a belief in Christ, which doth lead their hearts to
wander far from thee, our God ... And again we thank
thee, O God, that we are a chosen and holy people.
Amen." (Alma 31: 15-18)*

I like the way Alma's amazement was described, *After they
had heard these prayers* (and their mouths gaped open)
they were astonished beyond all measure. (Alma 31:19).
Beyond all measure! There was no way to be more
astonished. Poor guys! They must have been thinking to
themselves, "These people must be out of their minds!"

Although this missionary envoy is successful in con-
verting many Zoramites to the truth, their success is
mostly among the poor and downtrodden. The truly
proud and puffed-up people in the synagogues use
Corianton's adultery with the Harlot Isabel as an excuse
that the teachings of the missionaries are false.

The poor converts are rejected by the upper classes of
Antionum and are cast out. The Zoramites' rebellion is
completed when they do actually join forces with the
nearby Lamanites and stir up the Lamanites to fight against
the Nephites. The Zoramites are placed at the head of the
Lamanite armies (because of their bitter hatred for Alma
and other "religious" people) and a sore battle ensues.
Nevertheless, God is with the Nephites and the Zoramites/
Lamanites are defeated.

All of the Zoramite Captains are killed. Although there is no mention of Zoram personally dying in this battle, it is believed that he probably got killed in this battle.

What we learn from Zoram

- Zoram is a good example of how a conceited man acts.
- We learn how puffed-up people can become.
- We learn that much wickedness can be performed in the name of God.
- We learn the important role humility needs to play in one's life.
- We learn the sad consequences when one refuses to humble themselves before God.
- We learn that our pride, our stubbornness, and our conceit can have long-lasting, negative consequences.

Personal Application

- Are you conceited?
- Do you want to follow the commandments or do you wish the commandments would change for you?
- When you pray, do you dictate to God, or do you humble yourself before God?
- If the whole world could see your prayers, would they laugh at the arrogance you show?
- Are you satisfied with your life simply because there are others less fortunate than yourself?

Thoughts

The life of Zoram is scary. He rejects his religion, forsakes his countrymen, sides with the enemy, has the gall to place himself above others and God, and then tries to enforce his arrogance with the sword. He leads many thousands of people to their death with his phony zeal. Such a talented priesthood holder could have been a great asset to Alma and the Lord in bringing many people to the light of Christ. However, through pride and conceit, he falls all the way to the bottom! "Going down!"

Zoram

Now it came to pass that after the end of Korihor, Alma having received tidings that the Zoramites were perverting the ways of the Lord, and that Zoram, who was their leader, was leading the hearts of the people to bow down to dumb idols, his heart again began to sicken because of the iniquity of the people.

Now the Zoramites were dissenters from the Nephites; therefore they had had the word of God preached unto them. But they had fallen into great errors, for they would not observe to keep the commandments of God, and his statutes, according to the law of Moses.

Alma 31:1-8-9

6

Morianton

One of Three Run-a-ways

Alma 50

Born: Circa 71 BC
Raised: Most likely in Zarahemla. He would later move and settle on land nearby.
Religion: Doesn't say. He was most likely taught the Law of Moses as a youth.
Nationality: Nephite. Certainly not a Lamanite, living so far north.
Profession: Does not say.
Major Sins: Pride. Covets the land of the people of Lehi. Rebels against the government and the military.
Repented: No.
Result: Captain Teancum kills him as he tries to escape to the land northward.

Summary of Morianton

I was 18 years old when I first remember reading the 50th chapter of Alma. When I was finished, it was as if I could hear the voice of Joseph Smith whisper to me, "I'm not making this stuff up! You think I could make this up?" Reading it in 1984, it reminded me of a sappy John Wayne western or a dramatic Jimmy Stewart love story. But since the *Book of Mormon* was published in 1830, the movies actually came later.

So a Nephite man named Morianton moves with some friends and family west of Zarahemla to settle some land out by the city of Lehi. He colonizes the land and is quite successful. Soon, though, there are some arguments about where the two cities actually start and stop. Yes, this is a story of two feuding mayors over land rights. The town meetings don't remedy the hotly disputed town lines and a civil disturbance breaks out. The people of Lehi flee to the camp of a military leader named Moroni. Captain Moroni is called in to settle the dispute.

Morianton, sensing he is probably in the wrong, calls a meeting with his town's people and persuades them to come with him to the land North of Zarahemla where they can be in peace, which is better than facing Captain Moroni. They all agree. Here is the twisty part....

Let me just quote it for you, *And behold, they would have carried this plan into effect, but behold, Morianton, being a man of much passion, therefore he was angry with one of his maid servants and he fell upon her and beat her much. And it came to pass that she fled, and came over to the camp of Moroni and told Moroni all things concerning the matter, and also concerning their intentions to flee into the land northward.* (Alma 50:30-31)

In other words, Morianton beats up his girlfriend the night before they head out of town and so she runs to the sheriff and tells him of Wild Bart's plans of leaving town before sunup. Moroni sends an army to head them off at the pass, which of course they do, and in what was probably a made-for-TV ending, Teancum and Morianton (the two leading men) duel to the death. Teancum mortally wounds Morianton (hopefully in a dramatic sword fight).

The ending of the story has Teancum leading the people of Morianton back to the city of Morianton where they all vow to get along with the people of the city of Lehi. Lights dim. Show credits. (See Alma 50:30-35)

What we learn from Morianton

Morianton was stubborn and proud. He could not work out his problems peacefully and civilly. He had an opportunity to cooperate with the people of Lehi. He could have even cooperated when Teancum was chasing him. But he was stubborn. His stubbornness and pride led to the bloodshed and trauma of many people.

Once again, we see pride was this man's stumbling block. He had great potential to do good, and had even done much good in his life, but he allowed pride to get the best of him. He was jealous of what the People of Lehi had. He was unwilling to be generous and neighborly. If he had been humble and listened to the land disputes fairly, none of this would have happened. We never would have even heard of this Nephite rebel. I guess that is one way to get your name in the record books.

We also learn that spouse abuse is not a new crisis.

Personal Application
- Does Morianton's stubbornness remind you of anyone?
- Do you tend to be stern and unyielding?
- Do you always have to be right?
- Do you always have to get your way?

- Does your temper get the best of you?
- How would your life be better if you were less stubborn and more service oriented?
- Are you that insecure that you can't let the other guy have their way for once?
- Do you yell, scream, and hit others to get your way?
- If so, you may have Morianton-itis.

Thoughts

God will have a humble people. Either they will choose to be humble, or they will be compelled to be humble. Morianton was compelled. I like the word choose better!

Morianton

And behold, they would have carried this plan into effect, (which would have been a cause to have been lamented) but behold, Morianton being a man of much passion, therefore he was angry with one of his maid servants, and he fell upon her and beat her much.

And it came to pass that the army which was sent by Moroni, which was led by a man whose name was Teancum, did meet the people of Morianton; and so stubborn were the people of Morianton, (being inspired by his wickedness and his flattering words) that a battle commenced between them, in the which Teancum did slay Morianton and defeat his army, and took them prisoners, and returned to the camp of Moroni.

Alma 50:30-35

7

Corianton

One of Three Run-a-ways

Born: Circa 75 BC
Raised: Zarahemla.
Religion: Jewish. His father was a prophet.
Nationality: Nephite. Son of Alma.
Profession: Unknown. Fallen missionary.
Major Sin: Fornication. He slept with a Harlot.
Causes nonmembers to reject the message.
Repented: Unknown. The *Book of Mormon*
text does not say. After four chapters of his
father's preaching, he probably thought
twice about his moral behavior.
Result: Unknown. He is called on another
mission. He probably repented for a short time.
He skipped town on the next boat sailing north.

Summary of Corianton

Here we have another prophet's son gone bad. Corianton
was Alma's son. He was well known in the community
and was probably given every privilege afforded a
prophet's son. Perhaps that is the downfall of Corianton;
he was used to getting what he wanted.

The *Book of Mormon* text actually says very little about Corianton. We know when Alma went to Antionum to preach to the Zoramites, he took Corianton with him. Sometime during the trip, Corianton met a woman by the name of Isabel (only one of three women mentioned by name in the whole *Book of Mormon*).

Unlike most missionaries, Corianton took a liking to Isabel and lusted after her. The ensuing affair must not have been too much of a secret because the proud Zoramites mocked Alma and his son saying, paraphrasing, "Oh sure you teach that you are different, but look at your own son. He is immoral. How true can your religion be if your own son can't follow it?"

This behavior by Corianton must have been extremely disheartening to Alma. Alma responds with four chapters of preaching to his son (as fathers are want to do). Corianton appears to be humbled by his father's teachings. He is called on another mission. The last we read of Corianton is when he sails off to the land northward to take supplies to Hagoth and his people.

What we learn from Corianton

- Obviously we learn that it doesn't matter who your father is, we all must become personally converted to the gospel and internalize our commitment to what is right.
- We also see how damaging one person's behavior can be on a whole community not believing a missionary's words. Corianton will likely be held accountable for all of the negative press he caused for the church. If the Zoramites had been converted, many people would not have

been killed in the ensuing battles.
- Wickedness never was happiness.

Personal Application

- Who is watching you?
- Who depends on you to do what is right?
- If a loved one were to leave the church based on your behavior, how would that make you feel?
- If a school friend of yours was almost ready to get baptized and then saw your best friend smoking, and then decided not to get baptized, how would that make you feel toward your friend?
- Is your testimony based on other's behavior, or do you have a testimony based on the Holy Ghost testifying to your heart that Jesus is the Christ?

Thoughts

Members can be the greatest stumbling blocks to non-members joining the church. Be careful, you may be the only *Bible* some people read all day

Corianton

And now, my son, I have somewhat more to say unto thee than what I said unto thy brother; for behold, have ye not observed the steadiness of thy brother, his faithfulness, and his diligence in keeping the commandments of God?

Behold, has he not set a good example for thee? For thou didst not give so much heed unto my words as did thy brother, among the people of the Zoramites.

Now this is what I have against thee; thou didst go on unto boasting in thy strength and thy wisdom.

Alma 39:1-2

8

King Noah

One of Four Silver Spoons

Mosiah 7-23

Born: Circa 160 BC.

Raised: He was either born in Zarahemla and went with his parents to the land of Nephi. Or he was born in the land of Nephi after his parents arrived. Noah was raised by his parents.

Religion: He is most definitely Jewish. He was taught the 10 commandments as a youth and believed in the Law of Moses. However, he did not follow the teachings of Christ.

Nationality: His dad was a Nephite spy. Zeniff and his zealous followers left Zarahemla to go back to the original landing spot of their forefathers, Father Lehi. Although now inhabited by Lamanites, they wanted to live in the land of their First Inheritance. (Kinda like Texans wanting to move to Plymouth Rock, Massachusetts.)

Profession: Political leader. King.

Major Sins: Execution of a prophet of God (Abinadi). Pride. Cowardice. Total apostasy.

Repented: No.

Result: Burned at the stake by his own priests.

Summary of Noah

Here is a guy with a silver spoon in his mouth. His dad is a king. He was probably schooled in the best schools, went to church in the nicest ward. He lived among priests and prophets. He had everything. But something went wrong. You got it, pride! He allowed pride into his life. He was more concerned about what man thought than about what God thought. Noah wanted God to change his laws to match his wants, instead of the other way around.

After his father died, and he became king, Noah's true heart and character began to emerge. He was not a true follower of Christ, as was his father. He surrounded himself with like-minded priests and then he went on a rampage; he became an alcoholic, whoremonger, apostate, hypocrite, traitor, and murderer. Through his selfish desires, he allowed his military to falter and his people to be overthrown.

His story is a classic one. King Noah, while hypocritically sitting in the judgement seat, Abinadi, the prophet is brought before him and his so-called priests. The charge is treason against the government and for calling the people of Noah to repentance. (Something Noah's priests should have been doing had they not been out drinking wine and soliciting harlots in their spare time.)

The only redeeming quality Noah shows is that he wasn't rock solid wicked, shown by his pricked heart as Abinadi spoke. He was about to let the prophet go, but the priests puffed him up, appealed to his pride and Noah fell for it. He ordered Abinadi burned at the stake (Mosiah 17:1). A few days later, the Lamanites attack their city and the coward Noah tells the men of the city to abandon their families and high tail it out of town, which they do. The

Lamanites have mercy on the fair women of the city and do not kill them.

Meanwhile, the men of the city are held up in the nearby forest and start realizing what their fearless leader has made them do. They become wroth with Noah. They conspire against Noah. They tie Noah to a tree and light the tree on fire. A painful end to a pathetic man. (Mosiah 19:20)

What we learn from Noah
The life of Noah illustrates the popular phenomenon known as the "Bishop's Son Syndrome." He also teaches us volumes about the pride of man. Noah should have repented. He was privileged to have a prophet in his midst. He had been taught the truth. Yet, he rejected it all. He listened to his friends instead of listening to the teachings of his religious leaders. Even when the spirit whispered to him that he needed to change, he fell under the weight of his own self-serving arrogance.

Personal Application
- Do you have a prophet living in your midst?
- Have you been taught the truth in your youth?
- Do you listen to friends more than you take the council of your ward leaders? Does your own pride keep you from repenting and forsaking your sins? Has the Spirit touched your heart, yet you are slow to obey?

Thoughts
Had Noah been humble, teachable, and childlike, he could have flourished in that land and been a force for good in bringing the Lamanites to the truth. What a waste!

King Noah

For behold, he did not
keep the commandments
of God, but he did walk
after the desires of his
own heart.

And he had many wives
and concubines.

And he did cause his
people to commit sin, and
do that which was
abominable in the sight
of the Lord.

Yea, and they did commit
whoredoms and all man-
ner of wickedness.

Mosiah 11:2

67

9

Amlici

One of Four Silver Spoons

Alma 2-4

Born: Circa 90 BC
Raised: Zarahemla. Charismatic.
Religion: Was probably taught the Law of Moses as a child. Knew of Christ's teachings.
Nationality: Nephite by birth. Raised in political circles
Profession: Political enthusiast. Military commander. Mediocre sword fighter.
Major Sins: Pride. Vanity. Power. Anti-Christian attitudes and beliefs.
Repented: No. He never repented.
Result. He died while trying to assassinate God's prophet.

Summary of Amlici

Amlici was born in the Nephite capital city of Zarahemla. He was a light-skinned Nephite (see *Book of Mormon* Index: Amlici), taught in the best schools, studied the ancient writings, and learned the religion of the day. He was no doubt familiar with the teachings of the prophets. He was talented, well spoken, and charismatic. He very well could have been a great candidate for a missionary companion to Alma. However, something went wrong with Amlici.

When we are introduced to him in chapter two of Alma, he has already reached a high status among the people of Nehor. In other words, he was a Nehor (the anti- Christ) convert. Despite Nehor's deathbed confession that he had perverted the ways of the Lord with lies and trickery, it was too late to change Amlici's heart. Amlici was already smitten with greed, pride, and lust for power and political position. (Alma 2:9)

Given his many talents, he quickly rose to the top of that Order, and was extremely successful at deceiving people. (Alma 2:1) They wanted him to be the king. There was a democratic vote among all the people of Zarahemla. He lost. He became enraged. His people held a secret vote and made him their private king. As their new king, he ordered his followers, more than 12,000 people, to take up arms and kill those who opposed him. Alma, suspecting that Amlici might throw a military temper tantrum, is prepared to meet him and his forces. A mini civil war erupts. Alma defeats Amlici's followers. Those who are not killed, flee into the wilderness. Alma thought that would be the last they saw of Amlici. Perhaps now he would repent. Perhaps he would humble himself. Perhaps he would see the error of his ways and return to the teachings of his youth. That might have happened.

However, before the sun came up the next day, Amlici had joined up with some new friends—Lamanites. Together with the Lamanites, the Amlicites became even more hardened toward Alma and the people of God. They convinced the Lamanites to join them in fighting Alma's army. Amlici's followers fought ferociously, but God was on Alma's side. God strengthened Alma, and in a exciting sword fight, Alma slayed Amlici. (Alma 2:31) Alma goes on to defeat the Lamanites also, even though he is greatly outnumbered. The few Amlicites who remained alive, stayed with the Lamanites, cursing God under their breath, spiritually bankrupt to the bitter end. (Read Alma 2-4)

What we learn from Amlici

Amlici reminds me of a lazy lifelong member of the church who never lifted a finger to gain his own testimony. Surrounded by church members his whole life, he never found out for himself the true divinity of Jesus Christ. Once a divergent set of beliefs came forward, he fell, hook, line, and sinker. Even when his mentor was exposed as a fake and a phony, Amlici pressed on. Why? Perhaps his pride prevented him from admitting he had fallen for a shmuck. Perhaps he was afraid of being excommunicated from the church. Maybe it was just easier to forge ahead. Besides, he was popular, well liked, and had tremendous power over the hearts of many people, a temptation few men have overcome. (See world history.)

Personal Application

- Who is your Nehor?
- What lie are you using to justify your sins?
- Is pride preventing you from admitting you have been stupid?
- Are you so set on being popular, you are willing to go to hell for your vain ambitions?
- Who are you leading down a path of deceit?
- Who is watching you?
- Are you ready to be held accountable for their apostasy also?
- How do you compare to Alma?
- Do you go to battle at the head of your army,

or do you cower behind justifications, ex
cuses, and blaming others?

- Do you pray for divine help, humbling
  yourself before God, or do you rely on your
  own foolish traditions, philosophies, and
  wretched arm of flesh?

Thoughts

One thing I learn from Amlici's story is that you don't want
to mess around with a prophet of God, especially when
he has a sword in his hand!

Amlici

Now this Amlici had, by his cunning, drawn away much people after him; even so much that they began to be very powerful; and they began to endeavor to establish Amlici to be king over the people.

Alma 2:2

73

10

Zeezrom

One of Four Silver Spoons

Alma 10-15)

Born: Circa 82 BC
Raised: Probably in or near the city of Ammonihah
Religion: Jewish. At least, he was well versed in the Jewish Law. As an adult, he taught anti-Christian beliefs.
Nationality: Nephite.
Profession: Lawyer.
Major Sins: Pride. Anti-Christian attitudes and behavior. Apostasy. Caused the death of a multitude of believers.
Repented: Yes, after nearly dying from guilt. Was raised from his sick bed by a miracle performed by Alma.
Result: Fully Repented. Was blessed of the Lord. Became a missionary for the church.

Summary of Zeezrom

To fully understand Zeezrom, one must understand the city in which he lived. He lived in a city founded by a Nephite named Ammonihah. The village grew and became quite a marvelous city. In addition to a full coinage monetary system, they had advanced rules of trade, bartering, and lawyering. It was such a large city its citizens laughed when Amulek prophesied that Lamanites would destroy it. By and by, these Ammonihahites fell away from their religion. Their apostasy was almost complete when Alma arrived on the scene. There were, however, a few fence sitters. Amulek is called to help Alma preach.

Zeezrom is introduced to the reader during an Amulek discourse. Zeezrom was a famous lawyer in Ammonihah. We don't know how old he was, but we know he is a smooth talking lawyer. He was their foremost advocate and was accustom to stirring up the people. That is how he got paid: solving people's problems. Over the years, Zeezrom had grown very wicked. He became expert in the devices of the devil. His wish in life was to destroy that which was good. (If everything is good, who needs a lawyer?)

He engages Amulek in conversation in front of a large, anti-Christian multitude of people gathered to hear the two missionaries speak. Zeezrom's plan is to cunningly trick Alma and Amulek in their words, so as to lay a trap for them. Once trapped, he could cause the people to cast them out. He even offered Amulek money if he would deny the existence of God. (Alma 11:21)

Amulek is blessed by the spirit of God and perceives Zeezrom's thoughts. Zeezrom is astonished. Alma goes on to preach some of the most powerful discourses in all of literature on Jesus Christ, his atonement, the resurrection and the final judgment. Zeezrom is completely mystified. He knows Alma and Amulek are true prophets of God. His trickery and deceitfulness turns to humility and a sincere desire to understand the truth. His heart is softened and he converts to Christianity. One problem. Others in the group do not. Their hearts are more hardened towards Alma and Amulek. Zeezrom feels responsible.

The people scream that Alma and Amulek are possessed of devils. When Zeezrom stands up to defend the two missionaries, the people turn on Zeezrom. The crowd starts to throw rocks at him. He flees the city. He moves to the city of Sidom. He hears that the people of Ammonihah have burned and killed the believers of Alma. Zeezrom is afflicted with a terrible fever. His guilt has paralyzed him. He realizes his own sins, and also knows he is to blame for the death of hundreds of innocent women and children. He also assumes that the apostate Ammonihahites killed Alma and Amulek (Alma 15:3).

The story of the prison walls tumbling down and all of Alma's accusers being killed is famous. What is not so famous is that Alma and Amulek flee the city and also wind up in Sidom. Zeezrom hears that they are alive. He sends for the two missionaries. The two missionaries heal him. He becomes a valiant missionary. He never strays from his faith again (Alma 31:5-6).

What we learn from Zeezrom
- We learn that even lawyers can repent.
- We learn that money and power can corrupt individuals and cities.
- We learn that popularity, power, money, esteem, and fame all pale to God's word. Isn't it interesting that Zeezrom became sick with guilt. His guilt almost killed him. He had a searing conscious.

- Even puffed up rich people would give anything to be in good standing with God.
- We learn that one's own apostasy can lead to the apostasy of others.
- We also learn that our own apostasy can lead to the death of others.
- Religious conviction is serious business!

Personal Application

- Who are the Zeezroms in your life?
- Does a fellow Jack-Mormon negatively influence you?
- Besides your own ignorant pride, who is keeping you from repenting of your sins?
- If there were a whole city of you, would the city kill the believers of Christ and imprison Alma and Amulek?
- What have you been offered to live your mediocre life of fault finding and justification. Ten senine of Gold? A great job? Pornography? Cool friends?
- If the prophet were in town, would you have the faith to send for him and ask for a blessing?

Thoughts

The part of this story I really like is how Zeezrom is humbled by the pure testimony of a missionary. Who have you shared your testimony with lately?

Zeezrom

Now, it was for the sole purpose to get gain, because they received their wages according to their employ, therefore, they did stir up the people to riotings, and all manner of disturbances and wickedness, that they might have more employ, that they might get money according to the suits which were brought before them; therefore they did stir up the people against Alma and Amulek.

Alma 11:20

79

11

Amulon

One of Four Silver Spoons

Mosiah 23-24

Born: Circa 160 BC
Raised: Probably in Zarahemla
Religion: Jewish. At least, he was well versed in the Jewish Law. He believed in the Law of Moses. As an adult, he became a Jack-Jew.
Nationality: Nephite
Profession: Priest
Major Sins: Murder. Kidnapping. Rape. Pride. Slavery. Total Apostasy.
Repented: Not recorded.
Result: Unknown

Summary of Amulon

Amulon had a wonderful, colorful, incredible life. He is truly one of the most least talked about apostates of the *Book of Mormon*. This guy really had an attitude and happened to have the timing and luck of a card shark, and the cunning and charm of a snake. We don't know how old he was when he was in King Noah's court. He may have been born in Zarahemla and then traveled with Zeniff's people down to the land of Nephi, or he was born and raised in Lehi-Nephi, in the land of Nephi. Either way, we are first introduced to him in the chapters containing Abinadi's prophecies.

Amulon was a friend to Alma. He was a trained and learned Jewish priest. (Mosiah 23:32) He was royalty among his Nephite people. However, it is obvious that he is an apostate priest when he rejects the teachings of Abinadi. He was proud, powerful and cunning. He talked King Noah into executing the prophet Abinadi. Later, when the Lamanites attacked, he fled into the wilderness, abandoning his wife and daughters. His family was left to plead for their lives. The Lamanites did not kill the priest's families, but they did take them prisoner. Amulon was so angry for listening to King Noah, or perhaps so embarrassed and humiliated at his own cowardice, he masterminded the burning of Noah to a tree.

This guy was ruthless. He respected no one. He was successful in killing the prophet and then the king. He was now in charge! His next adventure included the kidnapping and raping of 24 innocent Lamanite women. Amulon and his wicked band of apostate priests attacked and kidnaped 24 Lamanite women while they were dancing near a lake. They dragged them into the wilderness, threatened them with death, forced them into some kind of mock wedding, and enslaved them into marriage! I guess if you have already set a guy on fire and watched him burn to death, kidnapping is no big deal.

Next, he showed his cowardice once again when a stray army of the Lamanites happened by and discovered Amulon and his small community. Again, Amulon sent a woman to do his pleading and begging. He escaped into the forest and once again left his kidnapped wife behind to ask the Lamanites for mercy. The Lamanite army showed mercy on the Lamanite women and actually, remarkably, showed Amulon many courtesies. In fact, Amulon really hit it off with this army. He joined them and traveled with them.

As fate would have it, they stumbled upon a city of Nephites. Low and behold, the leader of this little band of Nephites was his old priest friend, Alma, from his Abinadi days. In what must have been a humiliating twist of events, Amulon was placed as a King over Alma and his people by the King of the Lamanites. Amulon promised to let Alma's people go if they tell them how to get back to the Lamanite Capital. Having just come from that direction, Alma agreed to show them. As you might expect, Amulon then double crosses God's servant and keeps them in bondage.

A few years later, in what turns out to be a miraculous evening, Alma escaped with his people as God causes a deep sleep to fall upon Amulon and his guards. Alma returned to Zarahemla with his rag- tag group of converts and Amulon was never heard of again. Whew!

What we learn from Amulon
- If you are going to be a wicked apostate Jewish priest, you might as well be a really bad wicked apostate Jewish priest!
- It is possible to become hardened to all feeling.
- Satan rewards his minions — to a point.
- Women are better negotiators than men.
- Even church leaders are tempted and fall.
- Even anointed priests can be led away.
- One might even get away with terrible sins, for awhile.

Personal Application

- Even though you may have a high calling in the church, do you mock your church leaders?
- Are you vengeful, spiteful, and violent?
- Does your pride prevent you from seeing your own mistakes?
- Do you blame others for your problems?
- Do you trick others to do your own bidding?
- Do you take responsibility for your own actions?
- Do you lie to get your own way? Are you a covenant breaker?
- Are you a promise keeper?

Thoughts

Amulon was a wicked, cowardly, self-centered, arrogant traitor. Oh, and he murdered people on the side, too. He was disloyal, a lair, a cheater, a conniver, a coward, and an apostate. He was a moral opportunist, a snake charmer, and had enough charisma to be very dangerous. One of my only disappointments with the *Book of Mormon* is that we never find out how Amulon dies. I am confident that he got his just desserts!

Amulon

And Amulon commanded them that they should stop their cries; and he put guards over them to watch them, that whosoever should be found calling upon God should be put to death.

Mosiah 24:11

85

12

Nehor

One of Three Anti-Christs

Alma 1:1-15

Born: Circa 91 BC
Raised: Zarahemla, Nephite capital.
Religion: Was probably taught Judaism as a youth.
Nationality: Nephite by birth. Probably light skinned.
Profession: Religious zealot.
Major Sins: Murder. Anti-Christian attitudes and behavior. Apostasy.
Repented: Deathbed repentance.
Result: He was executed for the murder of Gideon, a capital offense under their law.

Summary of Nehor

Nehor was born in the Nephite capital city of Zarahemla (*Book of Mormon* Index Nehor (2)). He was most likely a light skinned Nephite, taught in the best schools, studied the ancient writings, and learned the religion of the day. He was no doubt familiar with the teachings of the prophets. He was talented, well spoken, and charismatic. He very well could have been a great candidate for a missionary companion to Alma. However, something went wrong with Nehor. Somewhere along the line, he decided to rebel against God. He knew the truth. He may have even had a testimony at one time. However, for whatever reason, he began to preach a more "liberal" religion. (Alma 1:2-3)

He taught that all mankind would be resurrected and return to live with God forever, no matter what they did. He taught that they should not fear God because everyone would have Eternal Life, regardless of their sins. This kind of philosophy is just what the itching-eared Nephites were waiting for. Although a religion teaching that regardless of your behavior, you will be rewarded with celestial glory could scarcely be categorized as a religion, many people were deceived that this line of rational made more sense than: faith, repentance, baptism, etc..

The brilliance of Nehor was that he took some of the truth, and mixed in subtle falsehoods, small lies, and minor deviations. It was so cleverly disguised, many Nephites were deceived. However, I personally think there were many that would have believed anything Nehor would have said, as long as he taught that they would not be held accountable for their misdeeds. The *Book of Mormon* describes this as "itching ears."

Nehor's demise is quite fascinating. On his way to preach a religious sermon to his many followers, he meets an old church member and military hero named Gideon. (If you remember, Gideon is the one who almost killed King Noah on the tower. He was the guy who helped the people of Limhi escape from bondage to the Lamanites down in the Land of Nephi. Basically, he was a rock-solid member. Some believe that he was a valiant convert of Alma's).

He and Gideon struck up a conversation. They started talking about religion. Nehor discovered that Gideon was a Christian and began to berate him. Gideon bore his testimony of Christ. Nehor became enraged at the truth spoken by Gideon. Since Nehor could not trick Gideon, he decided to kill him (Alma 1:9). He drew his sword and slayed Gideon. Nehor was caught. He was taken before Alma. Alma sentenced him to death (they had the death penalty back then). Nehor confessed that he knew he was perverting the ways of God. The people took him to Hill Manti and he was executed for the crime of murder. (Alma 1:14-15)

"Nevertheless, this did not put an end to the spreading of priestcraft through the land; for there were many who loved the vain things of the world, and they went forth preaching false doctrines; and this they did for the sake of riches and honor." (Alma 1: 16 and Chapter on Amlici)

What we learn from Nehor

This guy is a real gem. He teaches us that the "war in heaven" is still being waged in the first century BC. Lucifer's premortal plan was the exact doctrine taught by Nehor.

- No accountability.
- No wrong.
- Everyone saved.
- Everyone gets back to heaven.

This philosophy is rampant today and deceives many church members, even those who have felt the spirit, know what is right, but are proud and stubborn regarding their own sins.

We also learn that those people we deceive in this life may continue on sinning even after we have admitted our mistakes. To some degree, we will be held accountable for their apostasy.

Ironically, one issue Nehor does illustrate with his own behavior is the absurdity of his own doctrine. If there is no accountability for one's actions, what is to keep one from killing the guy next to you for not believing in what you do? It is not rational. It never will be. "Do what feels good" is a recipe for societal chaos.

Personal Application

- Are you willing to lay down your life for Christ even when a sword is to your throat?
- Do you wish God would change to meet your wants and desires, instead of the other way around?
- To which characteristics of Nehor do you most closely relate?
- Are you stubborn, selfish, hardhearted, and quick to anger?
- Are you proud, jealous, and judgmental of others?
- Do you seek popularity more than the truth?
- Do you seek money and honor more that the praise of God?

If you do, keep in mind what happened to the People of Nehor: "For the hearts of many were hardened and their names were blotted out, that they were remembered no more among the people of God"

Thoughts

Nehor is a great example of a bad man with a bad idea gone bad!

Nehor

And it came to pass that they took him; and his name was Nehor; and they carried him upon the top of the hill Manti, and there he was caused, or rather did acknowledge, between the heavens and the earth, that what he had taught to the people was contrary to the word of God; and there he suffered an ignominious death.

Alma 1:15

13

Korihor

One of Three Anti-Christs
Alma 30

Born: Circa 74 BC
Raised: Unknown
Religion: Unknown. As an adult, he taught anti-Christian beliefs.
Nationality: Unknown. Probably a light skinned Nephite. Doubtful that he would have been a dark skinned Lamanite strolling around Zarahemla preaching religion. Every other time a Lamanite preaches to the Nephites, the author mentions it.
Profession: Religious zealot. Anti-Christ.
Major Sins: Pride. Anti-Christian attitudes and behavior. Apostasy.
Repented:: Yes, partially, after being struck dumb by God.
Result: Was killed in the street by Zoramites

Summary of Korihor:
We know very little of Korihor's history. He was probably born and raised in or near Zarahemla. He was most likely a light skinned Nephite. He was taught the principles of

the gospel as a youth. However, sometime before arriving into Zarahemla, he had a very unique experience. He had a personal visitation from Lucifer, the devil himself. Satan appeared in the deceitful form of an angel. He "called" Korihor to be a missionary, to "redeem" the people. He taught Korihor exactly what to say. (Alma 30:52-53) Having been taught the truth as a youth, Korihor knew that what he was being taught by the angel was contrary to the teaching of God.

However, the teachings were pleasing to the carnal mind. In other words, they were easy to believe. Many believed his teachings. After telling the lies often enough, Korihor even started to believe them. After being kicked out of the cities of Jershon and Gideon, he was brought before Alma. Alma was astonished at Korihor's beliefs.

Summary of Korihor's Beliefs
(sound familiar?)
- No Christ will come.
- There is no God, and never will be.
- No man can know the future.
- Prophets are old men with deranged minds.
- Their dreams are whims.
- Christianity is the result of a frenzied mind.
- There will be no remission of sin.
- There is no wrong.
- All men should do what they want.
- There is no afterlife.
- Death is the end.
- Religious ordinances are a way to usurp power over people.

After committing blaspheme in Alma's presence, Korihor is rebuked by Alma's testimony. Korihor predictably resorts to a pathetic argument, "Okay, if there is a God, show me a sign?" (See Alma 30:49.) Alma says, "You want a sign? Okay. I will give you a sign. Shazaaam!" Korihor is made dumb. He is unable to speak. A fair sign for a man who used his language to pervert the ways of God. Korihor is astonished. He tells Alma of his visit with Satan. He admits he knew what he was doing was wrong. Alma does not remove the curse. Korihor is freed to go.

The rest of his life is a sad existence of begging and homelessness. The wicked people of Zoram eventually plot his murder. He is run over and trodden down in the land of the Zoramites. He died alone, poor, hungry, and a pathetic mute; killed by those who once puffed him up to popularity. (Alma 30:59)

What we learn from Korihor

- First of all, we learn Satan is real. He has great power to convince people of falsehoods.

- We learn that the people of Jershon (Lamanite converts) were not fooled by Korihor's lies, as were the Nephites. In other words, a strong testimony born by the spirit is your best defense against false doctrine.

- We learn Lucifer and false friends will most assuredly abandon you in the end.

- We learn that a sign isn't always what we think it will be.

- We learn there are very real consequences to one's own apostasy. (Death)

Personal Application

"And thus he did preach unto them, leading away the hearts of many, causing them to lift up their heads in their wickedness, yea leading away many women and also men to commit whoredoms—telling them that when a man is dead, that was the end thereof." (Alma 30)

- When you commit sins, are you humble or are you like Korihor, proud in your sins?
- Who are the Korihor's in your life?
- Who do you listen to?
- When you hear falsehoods, do you know that they are lies?
- What do you do about it?
- Do you shun the speaker?
- Run a way?
- Do you tie up the false speaker and carry him to your ecclesiastical leaders (like the People of Ammon did)?
- If you continue down the path you are currently on, will you end up alone and hungry for the bread of life?
- Will you be an outcast from those who love you?
- Is it really worth it?

Thoughts

I personally like Alma's logic in defending the truth. Consider these verses—with a little paraphrasing. (Alma 30:43-48)

Alma: Do you believe that there is a God?

Korihor: No!

Alma: I know there is a God and Christ will come. Do you

really deny the existence of a God, and the coming of
Jesus Christ?

Korihor: That's right! You have no evidence these things
are true! You can't prove there is a God! You have a
frenzied mind! I hate you and I hate your religion!

Alma: Okay, Korihor. You are so stuck on evidence and
proof, show me some proof there is no God. Give me
some evidence Christ will not come. Can you? Come on
Mr. know-it-all. Where is your proof?

Korihor: Uh, um, uh, well, um, uh ….

Alma: You don't have anything, except your own word. I
have all things as testimony that there is a God. The world,
the seasons, all creations, the prophets, everything!

Korihor: Um, uh, um, well, um … show me a sign and
then I will believe ….

Alma: Well, Korihor, you should be careful what you
wish for …. You want a sign? God will give you a sign …!

Korihor

But it came to pass in the latter end of the seventeenth year, there came a man into the land of Zarahemla, and he was Anti-Christ, for he began to preach unto the people against the prophecies which had been spoken by the prophets, concerning the coming of Christ.

And this Anti-Christ, whose name was Korihor, (and the law could have no hold upon him) began to preach unto the people that there should be no Christ.

Alma 30:6, 12

14

Sherem

One of Three Anti-Christs

Jacob 7

Born: Circa 500 BC
Raised: Probably in or near the Land of Nephi (the Nephites still lived there, too).
Religion: Jewish. At least, he was well versed in the Jewish Law. He believed in the Law of Moses. As an adult, he taught anti-Christian beliefs.
Nationality: Most likely Nephite. Possibly a Mulekite. He was not a Lamanite.
Profession: Religious Preacher
Major Sins: Pride. Anti-Christian attitudes and behavior. Apostasy. Tempted God.
Repented:: Yes, at his deathbed.
Result: Struck dead by God.

Summary of Sherem

Little is known about Sherem's past. He is a contemporary of Jacob, the brother of Nephi. We know he was not a Lamanite. He may have been a son of Ishmael. Since it was only 60 years since Nephi arrived in the new world, he must have come with them, or was born shortly after arriving. The strange part is that Jacob says, "there came a man among the people, whose name was Sherem ...." It appears as though Jacob did not know him. If Jacob did not know him, then maybe he was already here (possibly a part of Mulek's group). Sherem had heard of Jacob and his miraculous spiritual experiences. He sought an audience with Jacob. He may have thought if he could corrupt the prophet, then more converts would follow.

However, Jacob could not be tricked by such a rookie as Sherem. We do know Sherem spoke the same language as Jacob and was most expert in speaking. "... he was learned, that he had a perfect knowledge of the language of the people; wherefore, he could use much flattery, and much power of speech, according to the power of the devil ...." (Jacob 7:1-2)

However, Jacob had seen angels, had ministers from heaven lay their hands on his head, had heard the voice of God from time to time, and had the Holy Ghost witness to him of the truth of the coming of Christ. Sherem was out of his league.

Sherem's Doctrine

- There shall be no Christ.
- There shall be no atonement.
- No man can know the future.
- Prophets are mistaken.
- The Law of Moses will save the people.

Sherem tried to get Jacob to believe these false doctrines. Jacob simply bears his testimony to him of the scriptures, of the prophets, of the power of the Holy Ghost. Sherem was grasping at straws by the time he pathetically asked for a sign. (Jacob 7:13)

Jacob's response is classically apropos: "What am I that I should tempt God to show thee a sign in the thing which thou knowest to be true? Yet thou would deny it, because thou art of the devil. Nevertheless, not my will be done; but if God shall smite thee, let that be a sign unto you thee that he has power, both in heaven and in earth." (Jacob 7:14)

After saying this, Sherem is struck to the earth by the power of God. On his deathbed, he asks all the people who had believed in his false words be gathered together. With his dying breath, he confesses the devil had deceived him and everything he taught was wrong, there would be a Christ, and the prophets are true, etc..

Because he says this on his deathbed, the people are greatly astonished, and finally they repent. Sherem dies. His final words are haunting: "I was deceived by the power of the devil. I fear lest I have committed the unpardonable sin, for I have lied unto God; for I have denied the Christ, and said that I have believed the scriptures; and they truly testify of him. And because I have thus lied unto God I greatly fear lest my case shall be awful ...." (Jacob 7:20)

What we learn from Sherem
- Without a testimony borne by the spirit, it is easy to fall for false doctrine.
- Asking for a sign is mocking God!
- Signs are not given to convince anyone of anything.
- Deathbed repentance is revealed as only death

BAD BOYS OF THE BOOK OF MORMON

bed confession. There was a lot left undone.
- If you believe in the *Bible*, then you have to believe Christ will come.

Personal Application
- Who are the **Sherems** in your life?
- Do you seek for a sign?
- Do you lie to God by saying you believe in the scriptures, but then deny them with your behavior?
- Do you pick and choose which scriptural teachings you will follow?
- Does Satan have a hold on your heart?
- When you hear false doctrine, do you combat it with your testimony?

Thoughts
The best part of this story is the part where Jacob says he won't tempt God by asking for a sign to testify of something Sherem already knew. I think most signs we seek are simply to confirm something we already believe! We should simply act on the beliefs we already know to be true. Signs will do little to change us.

Also, notice how similar Sherem's teachings are to Nehor and Korihor's teachings. These guys lived 400 years apart. Satan has been preaching his same lies for centuries.

Sherem

And it came to pass that he began to preach among the people, and to declare unto them that there should be no Christ.

And he preached many things which were flattering unto the people; and this he did that he might overthrow the doctrine of Christ. And he labored diligently that he might lead away the hearts of the people, insomuch that he did lead away many hearts; and he knowing that I, Jacob, had faith in Christ who should come, he sought much opportunity that he might come unto me.

Jacob 7:2-3

15

Kishkumen

One of Three Dangerous Hypocrites

Helaman 1

Born: Circa 52 BC
Raised: Probably raised in the land of Zarahemla.
Religion: Was probably taught Judaism as a youth.
Nationality: All of his friends and family live in Zarahemla. He is most likely a light skinned Nephite.
Profession: Robber.
Major Sins: Murder. Conspiracy. Secret combinations. Thirst for power.
Repented: No. Died in the very act of committing murder.
Result: Died in his sins. Will most likely be unhappy with his final judgement.

Summary of Kishkumen:

Kishkumen is a contemporary of Helaman and Pahoran in 52 BC. He was a quick and speedy man who had a knack for talking people into making outrageous promises of secrecy—punishable by death. His family and friends openly agreed to hide Kishkumen, lie for Kishkumen and conspire with Kishkumen to assassinate the King. His Nephite family, was at the very least, two-faced, lying hypocrites, without the morale courage to stand up for the truth. They were really the ones who enabled Kishkumen to carry out his dastardly plan (Helaman 1:11).

The secret combinations and secret promises of his family and friends, and people like them, eventually become the root cause of the downfall of almost the entire Nephite nation. Kishkumen however, did not live long enough to see this. He was discovered and killed through a little play acting of another. It's funny that Kishkumen, the master of disguise and deceit, was out-tricked and out-deceived by a loyal and worthy servant of God (Helaman 2:8).

Background to Kishkumen's Fall

In 52 BC the political landscape in Zarahemla was in a perilous situation. The chief judge had died. There was strong arguments on who his successor should be. The people were hotly divided into three groups. Each candidate was a son of the former Chief Judge. A popular election was held and the winner was the oldest of the three sons, Pahoran. Pahoran was placed as the new chief judge and the runner up candidate acknowledged that he was beaten fair and square. However, the last place candidate was mad. He was a jealous little brother and wouldn't let it end. He became embittered. His lust for power and authority would not be denied. He gathered his followers together and emotionally whipped them into a frenzy. They plotted the overthrow of the government. But their plans were discovered and the brother, named Paanchi, was sent to prison.

However, this did not end the movement. It only enraged

them. They hired an assassin. You guessed it. Kishkumen! The fastest runner in all of Zarahemla. Kishkumen had his orders. He boldly went forth into the chief judge's palace and snuck up to the throne where the king was sitting with many servants, and in broad daylight, brazenly put a dagger into Pahoran's heart. The servants chased him, but he was too speedy. His disguise hid his appearance and he got away. He made a secret promise with the followers of Paanchi not to reveal that it was he. They all swore to the death.

Well, a few days later, the runner-up candidate, Pacumeni was placed in the judgement seat, as was their custom. However, Pacumeni soon died in a war with the Laman-ites. (Killed by Coriantumr when he stormed Zarahemla.) With son number one assassinated, son number two killed in battle, and son number three in prison, the people had another vote and elected Helaman, the son of Helaman, to be the chief judge. Well, Kishkumen lived through the war and now decided that he is going to try it again. This time he sneaked in at night, in full disguise. As he was wandering the halls of the palace looking for Helaman, he stumbled upon one of the servants. By some clever trickery of his own, the servant pretended to be one of Kishkumen's secret followers. The servant agreed to lead Kishkumen to where Helaman was sitting on the judgement seat. Kishkumen was exceedingly happy and agreed to the plan.

However, Kishkumen's happiness was short lived. The next thing Kishkumen felt was a sharp pain in his heart. He looked down to see a knife sticking out of his chest. The servant ran and summoned the army and they chase the followers of Kishkumen who were hiding outside the palace (actually the small band of robbers were now led by a man whose name was Gadianton—more on him later). However, Gadianton escaped. That was the end of Kishkumen, but not the end of the Gadianton Robbers.

What we learn from Kishkumen

- Wickedness never was happiness.
- What goes around, comes around.
- If you live by the sword, you will die by the sword.
- Two can play the pretend game.
- Just because you have friends in low places, does not ensure that Satan will not abandon you in the end.
- Political and societal peace is a delicate animal.
- Secret combinations are wicked and of the devil.
- You may be fast, but you can't outrun justice!

Personal Application

- When you think you are being clever, you are probably only fooling yourself.
- Do you think you can really fool God?
- Do you stand for what is right, or do you passively enable your family and friends to sin.
- Never promise to keep a secret before you know what the secret is.
- Peer pressure is real.
- Don't underestimate the power to be talked into doing something.

Thoughts

Kishkumen was a Nephite apostate who volunteered to commit murder in exchange for being lifted up and rewarded by family and friends. He gave up his life for the vain and frail things of this world. What a waste!

Kishkumen

Now when those people who were desirous that he should be their governor saw that he was condemned unto death, therefore they were angry, and behold, they sent forth one Kishkumen, even to the judgment-seat of Pahoran, and murdered Pahoran as he sat upon the judgment-seat.

Helaman 1:9

16
Gadianton

One of Three Dangerous Hypocrites

Helaman 2-6

Born: Circa BC 52

Raised: Most likely Zarahemla. He was close to the royal family.

Religion: The book never says. Was probably a Jew.

Nationality: Nephite. Was loyal to the political families of his day. It is doubtful a Lamanite would form a secret combination with other Nephites and be able to walk among the city undetected if he was a dark skinned Lamanite.

Profession: Robber. Murderer. Plunderer. Military strategist.

Major sin: Pride. Murder. Total overthrow of Nephite civilization.

Repented:: No

Result: The book does not talk specifically of what happened to Gadianton. His band is successful of nearly destroying the entire Nephite civilization.

Summary of Gadianton

Little is known about Gadianton's life before being introduced to the reader as the leader of Kishkumen's family and friends. He makes an evil oath with Kishkumen. If Kishkumen kills Helaman and his clan swears to secrecy with a death oath, and they also put Gadianton as King, then Kishkumen and his family will be placed in high places within the government. Although Kishkumen fails to kill Helaman, Gadianton is quite successful at his desire to be leader over all the nation. Most would think that Gadianton was a Lamanite, because of the treachery he thrust upon the Nephites. But he wasn't. He was a Nephite dissenter.

Like all the villains named in the *Book of Mormon*, Gadianton was a traitor to his nation, to his family, and to his religion. The only person that Gadianton was loyal to was the Devil himself. The Devil taught Gadianton the secret signs and tokens to be used in his combinations. The devil would sustain him. Gadianton sold his soul for power, position, and popularity — and it almost worked.

As Christ's arrival neared, a strange phenomenon swept through the land. No longer was it Nephite versus Lamanite. No longer was it light skinned against dark skinned. It was Gadianton robbers versus non-Gadianton robbers. Both the Lamanites and the Nephites joined together to sweep them from the land. However, Lamanites also joined the secret band of robbers and the civil anarchy that erupted cost the lives of thousands. It was only through the inspired work of political, religious, and military leaders who lived in the land of Zarahemla, that the Gadianton robbers did not succeed in overthrowing the Nephite society.

What we learn from Gadianton

- Entire books have been written on this guy and his secret society. Weeks of institute classes are spent drawing analogies between secret combinations and our current day.
- Suffice it to say there are Gadiantons who walk among us today.
- There are those who have sold their souls to Satan.
- We learn from Gadianton that the Devil is real.
- We learn what happens to mankind when the people do not follow the teachings of Jesus Christ.

Personal Application:

- Secret combinations are scary.
- They are real.
- They destroy lives.
- They are subtle and they will bring unhappiness to all who participate.
- What are your secrets?
- What are you hiding?
- What is it in your life, which if your mother found it out, would bring shame and humiliation to you and your family?
- Do you care more about yourself than those around you?
- Are the philosophies and teachings you believe authored by God or by a thief and a robber?

Thoughts

Stay away from gangs, cliques, secret clubs, and never swear to keep a secret, unless the oath is between you and God.

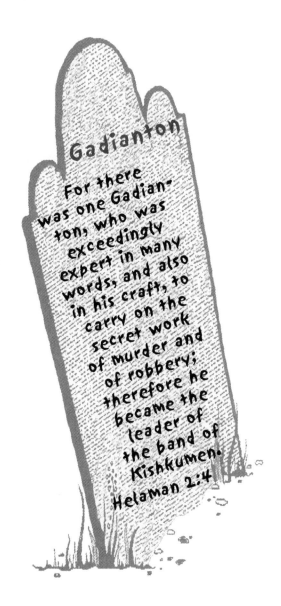

Gadianton

For there was one Gadian-ton, who was exceedingly expert in many words, and also in his craft, to carry on the secret work of murder and of robbery; therefore he became the leader of the band of Kishkumen.

Helaman 2:4

17
Seantum

One of Three Dangerous Hypocrites

Helaman 9-10

Born: Circa 23 BC
Raised: Zarahemla
Religion: Unknown. Gadianton Robber
Nationality: Nephite. Brother of Chief Judge of the Nephites.
Profession: Wannabe Chief Judge.
Major Sins: Secret Combinations. Murders his own brother.
Repented:: He confesses.
Result: He is arrested. That is all we know.

Summary of Seantum

As you can see, all assassinations, government over-throws, and political upheaval is caused, not by Laman-ites, but by Nephite traitors. Seantum is another example of a Nephite bad boy. His brother is the chief judge over the people of Nephi. Seantum wants what his brother has. Seantum enters into a secret combination. He plots the death of his brother so he can become the new chief judge. He goes to his brother at the judgement seat and slays him with a dagger to the heart. His brother falls to the ground and dies in a pool of blood. Seantum coolly returns to his own home and waits for someone to discover his assassinated brother. (Helaman 9:6)

Unfortunately for Seantum, the prophet Nephi uses the murder as a prophetic example of the wickedness of the people, and as a sign that Nephi is a prophet. While praying out on the garden tower, Nephi tells the people that even while he speaks, their chief judge is laying in a puddle of blood at the judgement seat. Sure enough, the chief judge is discovered to have been killed. Naturally, the people think that Nephi is a coconspirator. They arrest him.

Once again, Nephi must demonstrate his prophetic ability. He tells the court to go to the house of Seantum, the brother of the slain chief judge. He tells them to ask Seantum why he has blood on the hem of his coat. He also tells them Seantum will turn white and will look very scared and will then confess. The police do as they are told and sure enough, Seantum confesses. However, the police still think Nephi is in on it. They ask Seantum if Nephi plotted with him to kill the chief judge. Seantum, although a wicked, murdering Gadianton Robber, is astonished by the miracle and tells the police Nephi must be a prophet! (Helaman 9:37)

What we learn from Seantum
- Even as the demons that possessed the wild pigs knew Christ when they were in his presence, so it is with Seantum. Even a child of hell cannot dispute the power and authority of God. Why is it then that we are so reluctant to follow Jesus and do as he did?
- We also learn pride, lust for power, and

120

lust for control over others is a common, yet harrowing disease that has infected the minds and hearts of men for centuries.

- We learn time is relative and men can know the future, even down to the words that we will speak. How narrow and limited is our understanding of this life!
- We also learn those Nephites really had a dramatic flare for daggers to the heart!

Personal Application

- I know this is starting to sound like a broken record (the flat disks they used to play on phonographs that would get scratched and caused the needle to play the same sound over and over again). Pride is a great stumbling block to the members of the church.
- Do you have a thirst for power?
- Do you covet what your siblings or friends have?
- Do you go to great lengths to hide your sins?
- Are you waiting for a prophet to dramatically "out" you, or are you going to come forward and repent on your own?
- Which do you think is better?
- I think the Seantum story is amazing. We are so foolish if we think that we can fool God.

Thoughts

We are foolish if we think we can just "repent later" and all will be well. God knows what we are going to do, even before we do it. We might as well be obedient!

Seantum

And then shall he (Seantum) tremble, and shall look pale, even as if death had come upon him. And then shall ye say: Because of this fear and this paleness which has come upon your faces, behold, we know that thou art guilty. And then shall greater fear come upon him; and then shall he confess unto you, and deny no more that he has done this murder.

Helaman 9:33-35

Conclusion

There are many ways to teach someone a lesson. Some learn best through following a good example. Some learn best through seeing consequences of another's mistakes. The *Book of Mormon* teaches us both ways.

The seventeen Bad Boys illustrated in this book teach us through their bad example how not to act, not to think, and not to feel.

They also teach us

- When you pick up one end of a stick, you pick up the other.
- God is real. God is just. God is consistent. God will not be mocked!
- Pride is a deadly disease as real as any other deadly disease.
- Selfishness, vanity, conceit, and stubborn-ness, all come with a high price tag. Don't buy it!
- Personal testimony is the only defense to false doctrine, false prophets, and secret combinations.

- When sword fighting with a righteous prophet of God—you're going to lose!
- When you humble yourself before God and internally commit to follow his teachings, you're going to win!
- Satan is a real personage who has a long history of preaching, prodding, and persuading people to believe there are no consequences to sin, and then laughing his head off as we sin.
- Power, fame, popularity, blind ambition, and vanity are hollow counterfeits to love, hope, charity, service, humility, and faith.
- We can choose our friends. We can choose our behavior. We can choose our beliefs. We can seek for a sign. However, we can not choose the consequences to those decisions. The consequences are natural, eternal laws.
- Be careful what you wish for—it might not be what you think!
- What goes around, comes around.
- When you burn a prophet to death, you will be burned to death. When you stab a king in the heart, you will be stabbed in the heart. When you stab a High Priest in the heart, you will be stabbed in the heart ... Are you seeing a pattern here?

I am so thankful Mormon chose to include the stories of these Bad Boys. They are instructional, dramatic, and poignant. Much can be learned from their rise to popularity and from their fall to misery and death.

I pray we can be wise enough to learn from their bad examples and make all necessary adjustments to our own lives so as not to have to go down the dead-end path of disobedience, jealousy, and pride.

Consider the following scripture as it relates to our hearts. *"Therefore, he did stir them up to anger, and he did gather together his armies ... and did march down to battle ... and it came to pass that because of so much contention and so much difficulty ... that they had not kept sufficient guard ... for they supposed that they durst not come into the heart ... and attack ... but it came to pass that they did march into the heart ... with such exceedingly great speed that there was no time to gather together a defense."* (See Helaman 1:17-20)

- Watch you heart.
- Be prepared.
- The adversary will attack.
- Are you ready?

My prayer is that we learn from the mistakes of the bad boys and be prepared to withstand the attacks of the adversary.

Be careful out there!